Discovering Mission San Carlos Borroméo del Río Carmelo

BY SAM HAMILTON

Cavendish
Square

New York

Published in 2015 by Cavendish Square Publishing, LLC
243 5th Avenue, Suite 136, New York, NY 10016

Website: cavendishsq.com

This publication represents the opinions and views of the author based on his or her personal experience, knowledge, and research. The information in this book serves as a general guide only. The author and publisher have used their best efforts in preparing this book and disclaim liability rising directly or indirectly from the use and application of this book.

CPSIA Compliance Information: Batch #WS14CSQ

All websites were available and accurate when this book was sent to press.

Library of Congress Cataloging-in-Publication Data

Hamilton, Sam.
Discovering Mission San Carlos Borroméo del Río Carmelo / Sam Hamilton.
pages cm. — (California missions)
Includes index.
ISBN 978-1-62713-076-9 (hardcover) ISBN 978-1-62713-078-3 (ebook)
1. Mission San Carlos Borromeo (Carmel, Calif.)—History—Juvenile literature. I. Title.

F869.M653E34 2015
979.4'76—dc23

2014005335

Editorial Director: Dean Miller
Editor: Kristen Susienka
Copy Editor: Cynthia Roby
Art Director: Jeffrey Talbot
Designer: Douglas Brooks
Photo Researcher: J8 Media
Production Manager: Jennifer Ryder-Talbot
Production Editor: David McNamara

The photographs in this book are used by permission and through the courtesy of: Cover photo by UIG/Getty Images; Zack Frank/Shutterstock.com, 1; Jorg Hackemann/Shutterstock.com, 4; Courtesy California Missions Resource Center (CMRC), 6; Courtesy of UC Berkeley, Bancroft Library, 7; Ann Thiermann/Dancing at Quiroste/Ann Thiermann, 8; Buyenlarge/Archive Photos/Getty Images, 10; © 2012 Pentacle Press, 11; © 2014 Pentacle Press, 12; Universal Images Group/SuperStock, 15; © 2012 Pentacle Press, 17; Courtesy CMRC, 18; © 2012 Pentacle Press, 20-21; © 2012 Pentacle Press, 24; North Wind/North Wind Picture Archive, 26; Courtesy CMRC, 30; Everett Collection/SuperStock, 31; Courtesy CMRC, 33; Jorg Hackemann/Shutterstock.com, 34.

Printed in the United States of America

Contents

Mission San Carlos's church is decorated by artwork
made by people who lived there in the 1700s and 1800s.

4

1
Exploring a New World

Tucked into a valley about 6 miles (9.7 kilometers) from the Pacific Ocean stands a yellow building with rounded turrets and a wood door. This is Mission San Carlos Borroméo del Río Carmelo, one of the oldest missions in California. Above the mission's church door is a star-shaped window. Known as the Mudéjar Star, it is influenced by Middle Eastern architecture. This is a place with a unique and interesting story.

Built by Spanish **friars** (or *frays* in Spanish), soldiers, and Native Californians in the 1700s, Mission San Carlos Borroméo del Río Carmelo was the second of twenty-one missions founded by the Spanish along the coast of the Pacific Ocean between 1769 and 1823. The missions were intended to bring the **Christian** religion to the **indigenous people** and to increase the size and wealth of the Spanish empire.

EXPANDING SPAIN'S EMPIRE

The Spanish government sent men to explore the lands of the New World in search of riches, including gold. Their goal was to claim these new lands and any resources there as their own, making them the property of the Spanish empire. Several explorers sailed

Sebastián Vizcaíno was one Spanish explorer sent to the New World to claim land for Spain.

north from **New Spain** up and down the *Alta* California and *Baja* California coasts. *Alta* in Spanish means "upper," and refers to the land that is now part of the state of California. "Lower," or *Baja* California, refers to the land below it, reaching into Mexico. The new lands they conquered were named New Spain, and spread across modern-day Mexico and the southwestern United States.

In 1542, Juan Rodríguez Cabrillo sailed up the coast of California from New Spain to find a river connecting the Pacific and the Atlantic Oceans. Cabrillo landed in what would later be called San Diego Bay. He and his crew met local Native Americans and traded beads and cloth for food. Cabrillo described the indigenous people as friendly and peaceful.

In 1602, the Spanish government sent explorer Sebastián Vizcaíno to Alta California to search for new land. He discovered Monterey Bay and Carmel, where Mission San Carlos Borroméo del Río Carmelo would be located, and claimed the land for the Spanish empire. Reaching shore, members of the expedition went on land and held a Catholic Mass, or church service, under an oak tree. They named the area Carmel after Mount Carmel in present-day Israel.

2
The Esselen and Ohlone

When the first Europeans visited Alta California, more than 300,000 Native Californians lived there. The indigenous people of California were actually from a variety of different tribes. Each tribe had their own beliefs and cultural practices. They considered certain areas of land as their own territory.

Before Europeans arrived, Native Americans lived for thousands of years in California, each tribe with their own unique history, beliefs, language, and traditions.

Occasionally tribes would fight over the right to use these areas. The indigenous people who lived near Carmel were known as the **Esselen** and the **Ohlone**.

Not much is known about the Esselen, who were almost completely wiped out by the changes brought about by the arrival of the Spanish. Much of their culture is shrouded in mystery. As a result, most of the information we have about the Esselen is conjecture, or educated guesses. The Ohlone, however, had a much larger population than the Esselen, and much of their culture has been recorded, preserved, studied, and is even still practiced today. Much of what we know about both tribes we have learned from the history of the Ohlone.

The Ohlone were a large Native group in California that lived in villages where they raised families, foraged for food, and celebrated religious beliefs and customs.

HUNTING AND GATHERING

The Native Californians did not stay in one place. Tribes often had more than one village, and moved between them depending on the season and food supply. If one area became low on water, food, or building supplies, they moved to another area and gave the original site time to renew itself.

Both the Ohlone and Esselen hunted and gathered their food. They ate plants, nuts, insects, fish, and other animals. The Esselen didn't eat coyote or owl because they thought that these animals were sacred. They believed that people who died came back as owls. The Ohlone ate large amounts of shellfish and smelt, a type of fish that is plentiful near the Pacific Coast.

The men were hunters and fishermen. They used bows and arrows, traps, spears, and nets to hunt game and catch fish. They made tools and weapons from materials they could find near their villages, such as wood, grass, shells, bone, and stone. The men also wove nets out of long-stemmed grass or reeds they found growing near the water.

The women were responsible for gathering food and cooking. They collected grass, bulbs, seeds, herbs, roots, acorns, berries, and nuts. Acorns were a major source of nutrition for the Native Americans. They used mortars and pestles made from stones to grind the acorns into flour for bread, mush, and cakes. Acorns have an acid in them that makes them taste bad and can make people sick. The Native Americans had to leach, or wash, the acorn flour with water many times before it was ready to use. Women made baskets for leaching, cooking, storing food, and carrying water.

A WAY OF LIFE

The Ohlone wore few or no clothes in the warm California climate. Women wore apron-like skirts made of bark, grass, and hides. In cooler weather, and in the colder areas were the Esselen lived, people wore blankets or cloaks made of animal fur. Many Esselen and Ohlone painted their bodies for decoration.

Native Americans who were part of the mission system were expert basket makers and made many types of baskets to carry objects long distances.

Nature played an important role in the Native Californian religions. Animals, plants, people, and the land all held special significance. Each tribe believed in a creator, as well as other gods and spirits. They believed that these spirits were at work in their environment, and often took on the forms of things in nature, such as the sun, moon, and wind.

There were many ceremonies that included singing and dancing. Such rituals marked the beginning of hunting trips and warfare. Weddings and births were celebrated, and the dead were honored. Initiation ceremonies brought both boys and girls into adulthood.

Before the arrival of Europeans, the Esselen and Ohlone had lived this way for thousands of years. Everything for them would change, however, when the Spanish appeared and established Mission San Carlos Borroméo del Río Carmelo.

3
The
Mission System

Centuries before founding Mission San Carlos Borroméo del Río Carmelo, the Spanish began colonizing the New World. Throughout the 1500s, the Spanish explored New Spain, or modern-day Mexico, lower California, and the American Southwest. They established a capital in Mexico City and began missions. The Spanish wanted the indigenous people living in New Spain to adopt the Spanish

© PENTACLE PRESS

Mission life often meant the friars and soldiers taught Native people European farming methods, like how to plow fields and care for livestock.

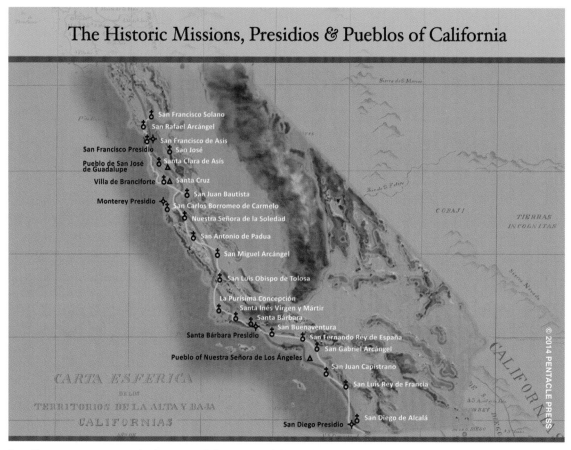

The Historic Missions, Presidios & Pueblos of California

San Francisco Solano
San Rafael Arcángel
San Francisco de Asís
San Francisco Presidio — San José
Pueblo de San José de Guadalupe — Santa Clara de Asís
Villa de Branciforte — Santa Cruz
San Juan Bautista
Monterey Presidio — San Carlos Borromeo de Carmelo
Nuestra Señora de la Soledad
San Antonio de Padua
San Miguel Arcángel
San Luis Obispo de Tolosa
La Purísima Concepción
Santa Inés Virgen y Mártir
Santa Bárbara
Santa Bárbara Presidio — San Buenaventura
San Fernando Rey de España
San Gabriel Arcángel
Pueblo of Nuestra Señora de Los Ángeles
San Juan Capistrano
San Luis Rey de Francia
San Diego Presidio — San Diego de Alcalá

CARTA ESFERICA
DE LOS
TERRITORIOS DE LA ALTA Y BAJA
CALIFORNIAS

© 2014 PENTACLE PRESS

In all, twenty-one missions and four presidios were established in Alta California from 1769 to 1823.

COLONIZING CALIFORNIA

The Spanish came from a world that looked down on indigenous peoples. They thought the people living in the Americas were "uncivilized" because they were not educated in schools, wore few clothes, lived off the land, and moved from place to place. The Spanish believed that it was in the best interest of the

Native Americans to live as Spaniards did, instead of the "savages" the Spanish perceived them to be.

By the 1700s, the Spanish government had procedures for building religious settlements, called missions, in New Spain. Soldiers and missionaries were sent to teach the Esselen and Ohlone about Spanish practices and Christianity. In addition, the missionaries taught the Native Americans how to grow food, raise cattle and sheep, and make tools and crafts such as soap, candles, horseshoes, and woven and leather goods. In the meantime, the soldiers began building **presidios**, or fortresses, to guard the land they had claimed for Spain against hostile indigenous people as well as other countries that also wanted the land.

The Spanish estimated that it would take ten years to train the Native Americans in Spanish work methods. After this time, the Spanish intended to return the mission lands to the Esselen and Ohlone to operate by themselves. The land would still belong to Spain, and the Native Americans would become tax-paying Spanish citizens. This process was called **secularization**. Once the lands were returned to the Esselen and Ohlone, the missionaries would travel to another area, build a new mission, and teach other Native Americans about the Spanish way of life and religion.

By the mid-1700s, many Spanish missions had been built in present-day Central and South America, as well as in New Spain. Then in 1768, word that Russia and England wanted the land in Alta California reached the Spanish king. He quickly decided to have a new chain of missions built along California's coast.

4
The Beginning of the Mission

In 1769, the government of New Spain sent land and sea expeditions to Alta California. Leading them was Captain Gaspár de Portolá, governor of the Californias. A priest named Fray Junípero Serra also joined Portolá to start the chain of missions. These men led friars, soldiers, and Native people from missions in New Spain to find new mission sites and build a presidio in Monterey.

FRAY SERRA AND CAPTAIN PORTOLÁ

In 1769, Fray Serra was chosen by church officials to be the president of the mission system planned for Alta California. During his fifteen years in Alta California, Fray Serra founded nine missions and **baptized** more than 6,000 Native Americans. As mission president, Fray Serra made his headquarters at Carmel but traveled frequently to check on the other missions. Today, Fray Serra is a candidate for Catholic sainthood, an honor given to someone in the Catholic faith who has devoted his or her life to God.

Captain Gaspár de Portolá led the expeditions to San Diego and Monterey and worked with Fray Serra to begin the Alta California missions. After many successful years in the military, he was named governor of the Californias. In 1776, he became mayor of Puebla, New Spain.

FINDING MONTEREY

Five groups left Mexico to set up missions in Alta California in 1769. Three ships sailed northward along the Pacific Coast. Two land groups traveled across the rough desert terrain of Baja California.

Fray Serra was the first leader of the Alta California missions and founder of Mission San Carlos Borroméo del Río Carmelo.

All groups were to meet near the harbor in San Diego.

The journey was difficult for everyone. By the time the explorers and ships met at San Diego, less than half of the approximately 200 sailors who started out on the journey were still alive. Once there, Fray Serra and some of the men started to clear land for Mission San Diego de Alcalá, the first of the California missions.

On July 14, 1769, Portolá and about sixty-five men left in search of Monterey, the spot that had been described by Vizcaíno back in 1602. Their first efforts to find Vizcaíno's Monterey Bay were unsuccessful. The expedition reached the area on October 1, 1769, but the landscape didn't match Vizcaíno's description—so the explorers weren't certain they had found it.

Portolá and his expedition arrived back in San Diego six months after they had left. With new provisions to sustain the group, the search for Monterey began again. After traveling for about a month, Portolá's group found the cross it had erected on its first trip to Monterey several months earlier.

Fray Serra arrived at the port one week later. The group chose to build Mission San Carlos Borroméo del Río Carmelo near a large oak tree that they believed Vizcaíno's group had used for religious services back in 1602.

FOUNDING A NEW MISSION

Fray Serra founded the mission in 1770. On June 3, with indigenous people watching in the distance, the settlers hung a bell in Vizcaíno's oak tree, and Fray Serra conducted Mass. A large stone cross, the symbol of Christianity, was brought. All the members of the group participated in raising the cross and a Spanish flag. Muskets and cannons were fired during the dedication of the new mission. A legal record was drawn up stating the formal founding of the site. Fray Serra named it for Saint Charles Borroméo, the Archbishop of Milan, who died in 1538.

As construction of the mission began in Monterey, Fray Serra and the other settlers discovered that this was not the best site for a settlement. The soil was poor, and few indigenous people lived close by. This meant that food would be scarce, and **converts** scarcer. Another problem was how close the mission was to the presidio. The presidio was filled with soldiers, some of whom were "leather backs"—criminals who were given freedom provided they

Every mission was founded by raising a cross and the lead friar saying a Mass of dedication, as depicted here in a drawing of the founding of Mission San Diego Alcalá.

became soldiers. It was not a good or safe environment to encourage the Esselen and Ohlone to join the mission.

On July 9, 1770, Fray Serra sent a letter to the **viceroy** asking to move the mission. Within the first year, Fray Serra received permission from the government of New Spain to find a better site. He chose an area 6 miles (9.7 km) to the south in the Carmel Valley, close to the sea. However, because of Monterey's strategic location on the Pacific Coast, the army continued to build the presidio there while the mission moved to Carmel. They believed that this was the best way to protect the area from the threat of other European settlers trying to take the land away from Spain.

Each day ringing bells signaled when it was time for the men, women, and children living at the mission to pray, eat, work, and sleep.

5
A Fresh Start at the Mission

Before building began, Fray Serra blessed the Carmel Valley. He called it the "Garden of God" because of its beauty. A Mass was held on August 24, 1771, and it was then that Fray Serra officially dedicated the new site Mission San Carlos Borroméo del Río Carmelo. After, the group started constructing mission buildings.

BUILDING THE MISSION

All the mission complexes in Alta California were required to meet standards set by the Spanish government. Each mission was to be built in a quadrangle—a square made up of buildings. In the center would be a courtyard, called a **garth**, or patio. Around the garth there would be living quarters, storerooms, workrooms, a kitchen, and a dining room. The friars' quarters were called the *convento*. A church or chapel was constructed in the northeast corner.

The first structures at the mission were made with log walls and **thatched** roofs. There were five sailors, three soldiers, and forty converted indigenous people, or **neophytes**, from Baja California working on these buildings. Within six months, the laborers had constructed a wooden chapel, living quarters, a storehouse, and a corral within a wooden stockade, or fort.

Native people who joined the mission worked very hard to build its structures using tools and resources around them.

Fields for grazing cattle and sheep were outside of the mission's walls. Mission San Carlos Borroméo del Río Carmelo would eventually grow to have two *rancherías*, Buena Vista and El Tucho. Rancherías were small ranches with stables and corrals. The rancherías also allowed the *vaqueros*—cowboys or ranch hands— to tend to the animals that grazed far from the mission. At one point, Mission San Carlos Borroméo del Río Carmelo had a herd as large as 10,000 animals.

RECRUITING CONVERTS

The indigenous people watched as the laborers gathered the materials needed to build the mission complex. The workers cut down trees using axes and saws made of metal. The Esselen had never seen such tools before. Some of the Esselen were curious to try the new Spanish tools and offered to help the newcomers. Once people expressed an interest, the missionaries and soldiers seized the opportunity to put them to work and taught them how to use the tools.

The neophytes quickly became an essential part of the mission. Soon they were planting fields of wheat, corn, barely, beans, and other vegetables. Although Mission San Carlos Borroméo del Río Carmelo did not recruit as many neophytes as other missions, at one point the mission had more than 800 people living and working there.

A CHURCH MADE OF STONE

When the construction of Mission San Carlos Borroméo del Río Carmelo was well underway, Fray Serra set out to establish more missions in Alta California. While he traveled frequently to other mission sites, he set up his headquarters in Carmel, with a small, private cell about one hundred yards from the church. With his commitments to other missions, Fray Serra needed another friar to head Mission San Carlos Borroméo del Río Carmelo full time. He put Fray Francisco Palóu, one of his former students, in charge. Palóu oversaw the construction of many more buildings and work-shops between 1771 and 1784.

Most of the structures were made of wood, but several, such as the kitchen, storerooms, and carpentry shop, were made of **adobe** bricks. Adobe is a mixture of clay, water, straw, and sometimes manure. It was packed into molds to make bricks. The bricks were then dried in the sun.

Fray Serra had many plans for Mission San Carlos Borroméo del Río Carmelo. He wanted to build a stone church, and ordered the quarrying of sandstone. Unfortunately, he never got to see his new church. Fray Serra died in 1784. When Fray Palóu retired the following year, Fray Fermín Francisco Lasuén took over leadership of the mission. He later became the new president of the Alta California missions, and continued to keep the California missions headquarters at Mission San Carlos Borroméo del Río Carmelo.

In 1791, Manuel Ruíz, a master mason from New Spain, arrived to build a new church to replace Mission San Carlos Borroméo del Río Carmelo's original one and carry out Fray Serra's plan. Ruíz chose to build the new church on the same site as the original church, where both Fray Serra and Fray Crespí were buried. By 1793, the building of the new church began with the help of Lasuén and the other residents of the mission.

The builders quarried large slabs of sandstone from the Santa Lucia Mountains nearby. They hauled these rocks to the Carmel Valley on *carretas* (wooden carts pulled by oxen or mules). Using the stone, they formed walls and an arched ceiling 33 feet (10 m) high. To seal the walls, they covered them with a plaster made of seashells. Clay tiles built by hand and heated in a hot oven called a kiln created the floor. Finally, in 1797, the church was completed.

6
Life at the Mission

Friars and soldiers at Mission San Carlos Borroméo del Río Carmelo and its presidio were far from their homes and families, and did not have the comforts they once had. Fray Serra's room at the mission was simple, with a wooden bed, a scratchy blanket, a table and chair, and a candle for light. Because of these conditions, many friars and soldiers there felt alone. They didn't have much contact with people who had the same background as they did. Their language was different than the ones the Esselen and Ohlone spoke. For this reason, it was difficult for the groups to communicate.

SETTLING INTO A ROUTINE

The missionaries taught the Native Californians about the Catholic religion, European agriculture, trades, ranching, and cooking. They encouraged the Esselen and Ohlone to work on the mission by offering them food and trinkets. The friars taught Bible lessons, conducted Mass, and performed **baptisms**, weddings, and funerals. Conversion was the most important duty for the friars. They believed that only people who practiced Christianity could go to heaven. The friars considered teaching the indigenous

Women often did most of the cooking, cleaning, and weaving for the mission community.

people about Catholicism to be a sacred duty that saved souls. They also tried to maintain good relations with Spanish military and government officials, because problems often arose over the treatment of the indigenous peoples and other issues about how to run the mission.

Missionaries kept annual records that were later stored at Mission San Carlos Borroméo del Río Carmelo. They recorded facts about things such as agricultural production, livestock holdings, and the number of Esselen and Ohlone who had converted to Christianity. The records show that in 1784, Mission San Carlos Borroméo del Río Carmelo harvested nearly 63,300 pounds (28,712 kilograms) of wheat, 72,000 pounds (32,659 kg) of corn, and 70,000 pounds (31,751 kg) of barley. In 1795, more than 875 neophytes lived at the mission. However, by 1834, the number had dwindled to 165.

Life at Mission San Carlos Borroméo del Río Carmelo was very strict. The friars were accustomed to rigorous discipline and expected the same from the neophytes. The Esselen and Ohlone were required to work most of the day, and learned to follow

Catholic practices that had little or nothing to do with their own beliefs or lifestyle. Many of them had trouble adjusting.

A NEOPHYTE'S DAY AT THE MISSION

Bells rang to wake mission residents around sunrise. Everyone at the mission assembled in the garth and headed to the church for morning Mass, prayers, and religious instruction. Breakfast was cooked by the women at the mission. Most meals consisted of *atole*, a mush of corn or grain.

Next, work assignments were given to the adults, while the children attended lessons. The Spanish showed the neophyte men and women European work methods. They taught the men how to grow crops and tend to fields. The men were also trained to be carpenters, blacksmiths, makers of adobe tiles and bricks, shepherds, and *vaqueros* who herded cattle. They worked to repair the mission and construct new buildings.

The Spanish instructed neophyte women in cooking, particularly how to cook in brick ovens. Eventually corn and wheat flour were used instead of acorn flour. The women learned to use Spanish looms to make clothing and blankets for everyone in the mission. They crafted soap from tallow—a type of fat from cattle that is melted, then allowed to cool and harden.

At midday, lunch, usually consisting of *pozole*—a stew made of barley, beans, vegetables, and meat—was served. After lunch until about two, everyone enjoyed a *siesta*, or rest time, before returning to work. The neophytes then worked until five. Another Mass was held once people returned from their work. Supper was followed by prayers, Bible teachings, and Spanish and Latin language lessons. Spanish was important to learn so that the neophytes could communicate with the missionaries, while Latin allowed them to study the Bible and understand the Catholic Mass. In the evening, the neophytes had some time for recreation. They liked to sing, dance, and play games of chance. Then it would be time to sleep. Each night the women went to bed at eight, and the men went to bed at nine.

The routine of daily life was broken on occasion when *fiestas*, or feast days, were held for births, weddings, or other celebrations. The Esselen and Ohlone ceremonies featured the traditional songs and dances of their heritage. The missionaries usually didn't stop the neophytes from conducting traditional ceremonies, even though such rituals contradicted Christian beliefs.

In the beginning, the language barrier and the cultural differences made it difficult for the Spanish and the neophytes to understand each other's religion. The friars knew that allowing the neophytes to continue their traditions would make adjusting to living at the mission easier. The friars made Mass mandatory, but allowed these ceremonies so that the neophytes would remain peaceful.

7
Obstacles at the Mission

At the mission, differences between the Spanish and Native American cultures made life difficult for all involved, especially the Esselen and the Ohlone. Every day, friars and soldiers enforced a strict schedule on the neophytes. The neophytes were expected to adjust to Spanish ways. Many had trouble following the strict lifestyle and tried to leave the mission. Unless given special permission, neophytes were not allowed to leave. Soldiers bolted the mission gates shut, yet some Native people did manage to escape. Those who did were tracked down, brought back to the mission, and punished by whipping. The friars felt it necessary to lock single and unmarried women and girls in their dormitories at night. Many neophytes felt they had been brought into the mission against their wills and resented the missionaries and soldiers.

Tensions were made worse by the soldiers from the presidio. While the friars were strict, their ultimate goal was to help the Native Americans. Some of the Spanish soldiers at Mission San Carlos Borroméo del Río Carmelo did not feel that way, and treated the indigenous people badly, abusing the women and beating some of the men to death.

A BILL OF RIGHTS

In the 1770s, Fray Serra traveled to New Spain to talk to government officials about the problem of soldiers mistreating mission neophytes. Viceroy Antonio Bucareli agreed, and Fray Serra returned to Alta California with a document from the Spanish government stating that the missionaries could take control of the neophytes away from the military. This document was considered a Bill of Rights for indigenous people in California. Unfortunately, many soldiers disregarded the order and continued the cruelty.

FOOD SHORTAGES

The first winter in the Carmel Valley was very harsh. There wasn't enough food to eat at the mission. A band of soldiers traveled south in search of food. Their efforts were rewarded near an area known as Obispo, the Valley of the Bears. The soldiers brought back enough bear meat to last until spring.

Although the residents of the mission planted crops of wheat, corn, and barley each spring, the soil at Mission San Carlos Borroméo del Río Carmelo was poor. Often it was too cold and foggy for growing wheat and barley. Harvests didn't produce enough food to keep the mission thriving in its early years. Ships found it difficult to deliver supplies to the coastal mission because of unpredictable weather and storms. In 1773, the crops did not grow well, and the people at the mission had to live on just ground peas and milk through the winter. The neophytes often had to rely on their previous skills of hunting and gathering.

By 1774, Don Juan Bautista de Anza established an overland route, which allowed supplies to travel on a regular basis from New Spain to Alta California. Meanwhile, other missions came to the aid of Mission San Carlos Borroméo del Río Carmelo, supplying baskets of wheat, beans, and corn. Eventually the friars learned enough about the environment at Mission San Carlos Borroméo del Río Carmelo to change their farming habits, and the crops began to improve.

DISEASE

Disease was another problem facing the Native Americans. For the first time, they were exposed to all sorts of new diseases, such as measles, smallpox, chicken pox, and syphilis. The Spanish people had developed resistance to many of these diseases and rarely died from them, but the Native Americans' bodies had not developed any resistance to them. Many of the indigenous people throughout Alta California became sick and died from European diseases that their immune systems were not equipped to fight.

The neophytes' living conditions also caused disease. Women were locked in overcrowded, damp dormitories. Poor ventilation and improper sanitation systems contributed to the problem, making many of the neophytes sick, as well as attracting bugs and rats.

ATTACKED BY PIRATES

In October 1818, two ships arrived at Monterey Bay. They were led by the privateer Hippolyte de Bouchard. Bouchard wanted to

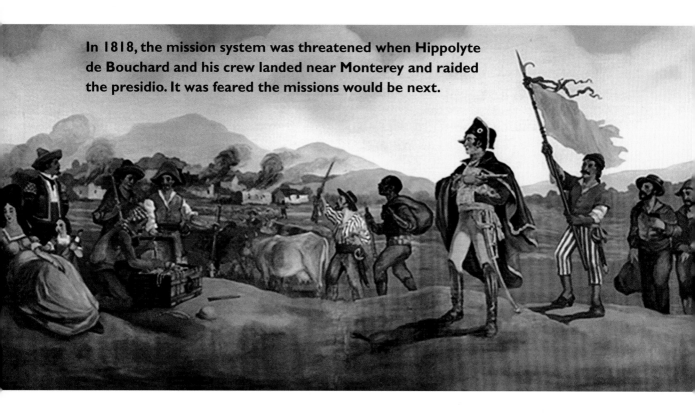

In 1818, the mission system was threatened when Hippolyte de Bouchard and his crew landed near Monterey and raided the presidio. It was feared the missions would be next.

raid the Spanish settlement at Mission San Carlos Borroméo del Río Carmelo. He and pirate Peter Corney sailed up to the presidio. Then their ships, the *Argentina* and *Santa Rosa*, began firing on the presidio.

The Spanish soldiers were prepared. They fired back on the pirates, and forced them to surrender and flee out to sea. Then the pirates attacked again, this time on foot. The Spanish soldiers were forced to run as 400 pirates captured the presidio's cannons. The friars and neophytes knew they had to leave and evacuated the mission to a safe place called San Clemente, where Rancho San Carlos is today. Bouchard, Corney, and their men looted the presidio and set fire to the fortress, but they left Mission San Carlos Borroméo del Río Carmelo intact.

8
Secularization

While life at the mission was difficult, New Spain was facing problems of its own. Some people living in New Spain wanted it to be its own country. In 1810, a civil war broke out between Spain and New Spain. Eleven years of fighting led to New Spain, renamed Mexico, gaining its independence in 1821. This meant they also controlled the Spanish missions.

The Mexicans had different ideas about the missions than the Spanish. They felt that the missions took up too much land, cost

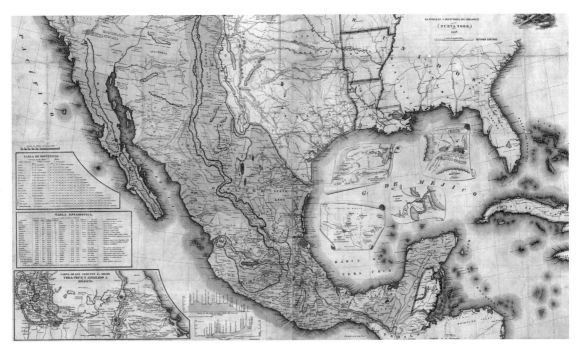

After winning independence in 1821, the Mexican government held great amounts of land once controlled by the Spanish.

too much money, and used neophytes without paying them. In 1826, Mexico passed laws to **emancipate**, or free, all neophytes in the mission system. Although now free to leave the missions, many neophytes were so used to mission life that they were afraid to go.

Fray José Reál arrived to oversee operations at Mission San Carlos Borroméo del Río Carmelo in 1834. In August of that same year, secularization laws finally went into effect in California. Originally the Spanish had planned to secularize the missions after ten years of operation. However, the friars had kept control of the missions rather than secularizing them. They believed that people still needed educating in the ways of the Spanish religion and culture and were not ready to run the missions on their own.

Though secularization was intended to distribute the mission lands, buildings, and livestock to the neophytes, most of the mission lands ended up in the hands of Mexican and Spanish landowners. Many neophytes left Mission San Carlos Borroméo del Río Carmelo and moved into the community surrounding the presidio at Monterey, becoming vaqueros or ranch hands.

Mexico's hold on Alta California lasted only a few years. American settlers from the east soon began moving into the area. The U.S. government eventually decided that it wanted to own the land of Alta California and fought with Mexico over control of it. The Americans won the war in 1848. The land now belonged to the U.S. government. Shortly after, miners discovered gold in California and thousands of settlers rushed there hoping to find riches. Then, in 1850, Alta California became the thirty-first state and was renamed California.

Secularization greatly affected the mission system and left many missions, including San Carlos Borroméo del Río Carmelo, in ruins.

In the 1850s, the U.S. Federal Land Commission returned some of the mission lands to the Roman Catholic Church. The church, convento, and several other buildings at Mission San Carlos Borroméo del Río Carmelo were returned to the Catholic Church by U.S. president James Buchanan in 1859. By then, the church roof had collapsed, exposing the interior walls to the weather, and the church became a **sanctuary** for birds, squirrels, cattle, and other wildlife.

Today many buildings at the mission have been restored, the mission church acts as a minor basilica, and its museum preserves artifacts and information on California's early history.

9
Mission San Carlos Borroméo Today

During the 1880s, missionaries began restoring Mission San Carlos Borroméo del Río Carmelo. However, it was not until Henry "Harry" Downie began restoring San Carlos in 1931 that the mission was brought back to its full grandeur.

BACK TO THE ORIGINAL

The church was restored, with a replica of its original altar. To recreate the original look, the church was decorated with brightly colored designs and artwork. The painted designs in the church at Mission San Carlos Borroméo del Río Carmelo had been mostly floral or geometric shapes. The ceiling of the church had a floral design. Now, half-circle patterns are painted on the arched roof supporting the choir loft. Also, triangles of green and white form a pattern along the sidewalls of the church. The church is also an important burial site. Below the sanctuary floor are the graves of the early mission fathers, including Fray Serra, Fray Crespí, Fray Lopez, and Fray Lasuén.

In 1961, Pope John XXIII designated the church as a minor basilica, an honor that elevates its status as a house of worship.

Mission San Carlos Borroméo del Río Carmelo is now one of the most popular religious sites in the United States. Visitors come from around the world to tour the restored mission complex.

Using documents written by Fray Palóu in 1784, Downie was able to recreate Fray Serra's room, the library, and the kitchen located in the northeast corner of the convento. This area now serves as a museum. The preservations shed light on some of the most important parts of California's history. For example, Mission San Carlos Borroméo del Río Carmelo is the site of California's first library. Originally the library contained only the books that Fray Serra brought with him on his first journey to Alta California in 1769. By 1820, nearly 2,000 books were housed in the mission's library.

BEYOND THE MISSION

The Monterey Peninsula has continued to thrive since Mission San Carlos Borroméo del Río Carmelo was founded there. The harvesting of sardines, first begun by the indigenous people of California, became a major industry along Monterey's Cannery Row. The presidio at Monterey is now home to two important schools, the U.S. Naval Postgraduate School and the Defense Language Institute. The Royal Presidio Chapel has continued to serve as a parish church since its founding in 1794.

The missions have molded the cultural and historical identity of the state. Mission San Carlos Borroméo del Río Carmelo reminds visitors and residents of the Carmel Valley of the struggles and hardships that made California what it is today.

10
Make Your Own Mission Model

**To make your own model of
Mission San Carlos Borroméo del Río Carmelo, you will need:**

- Three 20" × 20" pieces of Foam Core board
- ruler
- X-ACTO® knife (ask for an adult's help)
- glue
- pins

- light brown paint
- reddish-brown paint
- green and white paint
- uncooked lasagna
- masking tape
- colorful tissue paper

DIRECTIONS

Adult supervision is suggested.

Step 1: To make the base, cut a Foam Core board rectangle that measures 20" × 15" (50.8 cm × 38.1 cm). Paint with green paint. Let dry.

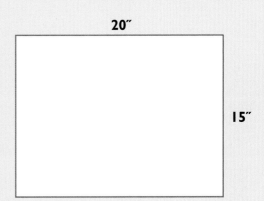

20˝

15˝

Step 2: Cut two 8.5" × 10" (21.6 cm x 25.4 cm) pieces of Foam Core board for the front and back of the church.

Step 3: Take one of these pieces and cut out windows and a rounded doorway.

Step 4: At the top of the front of the church, cut the Foam Core Board in the shape of a dome.

Step 5: Cut two 10" × 4" (25.4 cm × 10.2 cm) pieces of Foam Core board for the sides of the church building.

Step 6: Glue the front, back, and side walls of the church together. Stick the walls together with pins until the glue dries.

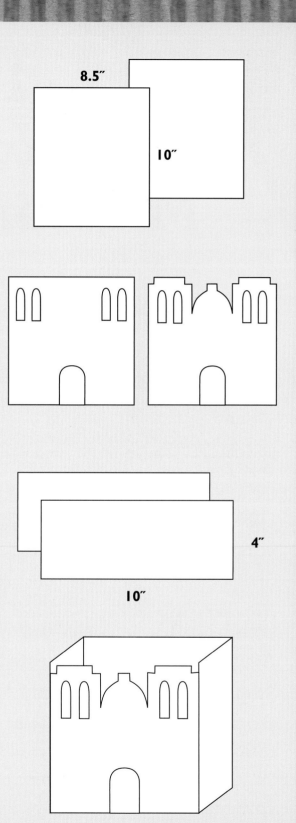

Step 7: Cut two 9" × 5" (22.9 cm × 12.7 cm) Foam Core board pieces for the inner walls of the quadrangle building. Cut two 11" × 5" (27.9 cm × 12.7 cm) pieces for the outer walls.

Step 8: Cut two 3" × 6.5" (7.6 cm × 16.5 cm) pieces of Foam Core board for the side walls of the mission quadrangle buildings. Cut the corners out as shown.

Step 9: Make the quadrangle buildings by gluing an inner wall (shorter) and an outer wall (longer) to each end piece. Pin them until the glue dries. Each structure will only have three sides and be mirror opposites of each other.

Step 10: Paint the church and the quadrangle buildings light brown, and let dry.

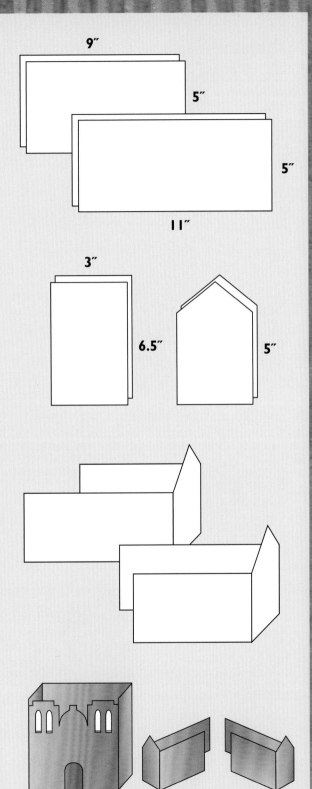

Step 11: Glue the quadrangle walls to the church. The open space of each rectangle should be attached to one of the side walls of the church. Pin the walls until the glue dries.

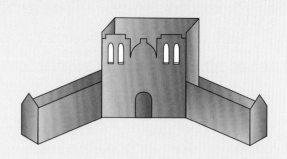

Step 12: Glue the church and quadrangle walls to the cardboard base.

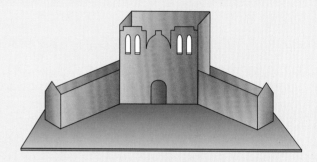

Step 13: Paint lasagna noodles reddish-brown and let dry. These will be the tiled roofs of the mission quadrangle walls.

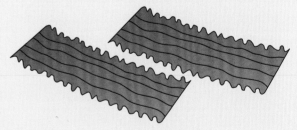

Step 14: Glue the lasagna noodles to the tops of each wall.

Step 15: Use the tissue paper to make small flowers and trees, and use these to decorate the mission courtyard.

The model of Mission San Carlos Borroméo del Río Carmelo when it is completed.

Key Dates in Mission History

1492	Christopher Columbus reaches the West Indies
1542	Cabrillo's expedition to California
1602	Sebastián Vizcaíno sails to California
1713	Fray Junípero Serra is born
1769	Founding of San Diego de Alcalá
1770	Founding of San Carlos Borroméo del Río Carmelo
1771	Founding of San Antonio de Padua and San Gabriel Arcángel
1772	Founding of San Luis Obispo de Tolosa
1775–76	Founding of San Juan Capistrano
1776	Founding of San Francisco de Asís
1776	Declaration of Independence is signed

1777	Founding of Santa Clara de Asís
1782	Founding of San Buenaventura
1784	Fray Serra dies
1786	Founding of Santa Bárbara
1787	Founding of La Purísima Concepción
1791	Founding of Santa Cruz and Nuestra Señora de la Soledad
1797	Founding of San José, San Juan Bautista, San Miguel Arcángel, and San Fernando Rey de España
1798	Founding of San Luis Rey de Francia
1804	Founding of Santa Inés
1817	Founding of San Rafael Arcángel
1823	Founding of San Francisco Solano
1833	Mexico passes Secularization Act
1848	Gold found in northern California
1850	California becomes the thirty-first state

Glossary

adobe (ah-DOH-bee) Sun-dried bricks made of straw, mud, and sometimes manure.

baptize (BAP-tyz) An act or ceremony performed when someone is accepted into, or accepts, the christian faith.

Christian (KRIS-chun) Someone who follows the Christian religion, or the teachings of Jesus Christ and the Bible.

convert (kun-VURT) To change religious beliefs.

emancipate (ih-man-sih-payt) To give freedom to.

Esselen (EH-suh-len) Native Americans who lived in the Carmel area when the Spanish first arrived in California.

friar (FRY-ur) A brother in a communal religious order. Friars also can be priests.

garth (GARTH) A courtyard within the walls of a mission, usually surrounded by the convento.

indigenous people (in-DIJ-en-us PEA-pel) People native born to a particular region or environment.

neophyte (NEE-oh-fyt) The name for a Native American once he or she was baptized into the Christian faith.

New Spain (NOO SPAYN) The area where the Spanish colonists had their capital in North America, and that would later become Mexico.

Ohlone (oh-LOH-nee) Native Americans that lived in the Monterey area when the Spanish arrived.

presidio (preh-SIH-dee-oh) A Spanish military fort.

sanctuary (SANK-choo-war-ee) A sacred part of a church containing the altar.

secularization (seh-kyoo-lur-ih-ZAY-shun) A process by which the mission lands were made to be nonreligious.

thatch (THACH) Twigs, grass, and bark bundled together.

viceroy (VYS-roy) A government official who rules an area as a representative of the king.

Pronunciation Guide

atole (ah-TOH-lay)

carretas (kah-RAY-tahs)

convento (kom-BEN-toh)

fiesta (fee-ES-tah)

fray (FRAY)

Ohlone (oh-LOH-nee)

pozole (poh-SOH-lay)

rancherías (rahn-cheh-REE-ahs)

siesta (see-EHS-tah)

vaqueros (bah-KEH-rohs)

Find Out More

To learn more about the missions of California, check out these books and websites:

BOOKS

Abbink, Emily. *Monterey Bay Area Missions*. Minneapolis, MN: Lerner Publishing, 2008.

Gibson, Karen Bush. *Native American History for Kids*. Chicago: Chicago Review Press, 2010.

Mission San Carlos Borroméo pamphlet. Carmel, CA: Carmel Mission Gift Shop.

Williams, Jack S. *The Ohlone of California*. New York, NY: PowerKids Press, 2003.

WEBSITES

California Mission Foundation

www.californiamissionsfoundation.org

This website provides quick and easy facts for the missions of Alta California and discusses the organization that preserves and protects the missions today.

California Missions Resource Center

www.missionscalifornia.com

This website gives essential facts about each mission. It also provides a timeline and a photo gallery, as well as detailed information about specific missions and the people who lived there.

California Mission Studies Association

www.californiamissionstudies.com

This is the website of the California Mission Studies Association, which has many useful articles and information about preservation efforts.

Monterey County Historical Society

www.mchsmuseum.com/carmelmission.html

To learn more about Mission San Carlos Borroméo del Río Carmelo, check out the Monterey County Historical Society website.

Index

Page numbers in **boldface** are illustrations.